A Rainbow of Hope

Stories and Activities to Help
Children Cope with Grief and Loss Issues

By Linda Hagler, M.Ed.

Cover Design & Layout by Elizabeth Madden
Project Editing by Susan Bowman & Renee Reasinger
Project Review by Cynthia Blakeslee

ISBN - 1-889636-31-2

Library of Congress Number
00-100512

10 9 8 7 6 5 4 3 2 1
Printed in the United States

Dedications

I Like It Here Just Fine is dedicated to Mama who worked so hard to make our house a home.

I Grew in Mommy's Heart is dedicated to birth mothers who choose adoption for their babies. May their hearts and lives be filled with the same love they give to the adoptive parents.

Ashes and More Ashes is dedicated to the volunteer firemen of our country who give unselfishly to their community.

Take Her Back is dedicated to my husband, Robert, for all his support and encouragement.

The Brown Suitcase is dedicated to my grandchildren Trace, Savanna and Hannah. May they visit often.

The Dinosaur Tamer is dedicated to Todd for his compassion toward others.

My New Foster Home is dedicated to foster parents for their contributions to the lives of children.

Buddy Was My Best Friend is dedicated to Andy and Wayne who understand puppy love.

Rocking, Rocking, Rocking is dedicated to Jeff Len Knudsen April 23, 1981-April 14, 1990.

I would like to dedicate *The Fresh Earth* to the memory of Daddy, a common working man, who loved his family and the smell of the freshly opened earth.

Linda Hagler

Table of Contents

Introduction

WELCOME! This series of books and activities was written with much love and concern for our children as they experience life and its many joys and sorrows. It is my heart's desire that the books will be read by students discovering their emotions or, perhaps, needing encouragement who can identify with the books' characters. In addition to the students, I hope the materials will be utilized by teachers and school counselors who are helping students deal with developing emotions, and parent(s) who are seeking ways to help their young children develop into well-rounded physically and emotionally healthy individuals.

How to Use This Program

The program is designed to be used in several ways. It has individual stories of children in crisis situations that can be easily read by children in the upper elementary grades or shared orally in the lower elementary grades. Written at the end of each story are thought provoking questions for the students. The program is also designed to be used by parent(s) or educators, in classrooms or group counseling settings with varied questions and activities to help children explore, understand, and better deal with grief and loss in their lives.

CAUTION

As you read these stories there may be some children who are going through similar experiences at home. These children may not want to share these private experiences in front of their peers. Invite students who need to talk about a specific concern to either meet with you after class or see the guidance counselor or social worker. Let the student know that you care about him/her very much. If he/she tells you about a situation involving danger or possible danger to him/her or others, you must report it to the proper authorities.

Due to the sensitive emotions involved with grief and loss and the varied backgrounds of the student population, it is suggested that parent(s) of the children be informed prior to beginning the sessions. A sample informational letter explaining the study is found on the following page.

Suggested activities involving field trips away from the school campus should be done only after obtaining parental permission for the field trip.

Dear Parents:

Grief and loss affect a child in all areas of his/her life. The methods used to cope with grief and loss in a child's life can help him/her develop into a productive, compassionate individual. However, if the child is not encouraged to deal with the grief and loss in a positive manner, he/she may become angry, aggressive, and sometimes explosive in later life.

A study of grief and loss issues is planned. Included in the study will be these issues: moving, adoption, loss of a home due to fire, a new baby in the home, divorce, dealing with a bully, foster care, death of a pet, death of a classmate and death of a parent. With each topic, a book will be shared and the students will be given opportunities to react to and discuss the book. Then selected activities will be used to help the students learn healthy coping skills.

In the event that your child has personally dealt with any of the issues, please list those on the letter so extra sensitivity can be shown to him/her.

Yours truly,

My child, _____, has permission to participate in the grief and loss sessions.

_____

Parent Signature

My child has personally dealt with these issues of grief and loss:

_____   _____

_____   _____

_____   _____

Why Focus on Grief and Loss?

Grief and loss are part of every individual's life. As we adults ponder our formative years, we do not always remember our many and varied experiences with grief and loss. Often, we exhaust much time and energy putting bad experiences behind us or suppressing them into our subconscious minds as we attempt to forget them. Instead of forgetting, the events and the involved emotions are often "bandaged" over, leaving underneath a scar that lives with us throughout our lifetime. The grief process is based on the theory of attachment and bonding. There may have been full attachment to the lost person or object or there may have been failure to attach. In either case, there will still be a sense of loss and a reaction to that loss.

To deal with reactions to that loss there are three options:

1. The loss may be denied and the individual may go on as if nothing happened and often paying a social and emotional price and even later experiencing many physical problems.

2. The individual may get stuck in the loss cycle and go over the experience again and again in flashbacks.

3. The individual may choose to resolve the loss and find new meaning in relationships with other persons or objects. (Childs, Gowell, 1992).

As we bury into our subconscious minds the experiences involving grief and loss, we often rob ourselves of important memories. All individuals carry emotional baggage or memories of past events that impact the present and the future. Adults just do not have to carry the baggage as far as children.

The early days and weeks of grief work for children may be compared to packing emotional suitcases as in these examples:

1. Unconsciously each feeling and thought is examined before it is packed into that emotional suitcase.

2. Sometimes it's easier for the children to cram all the emotions into the emotional suitcase and try to shut it as soon as possible without looking at what they have to carry. Unless

they are very careful, the feelings like the over packed suitcase, hang out caught in the sides. Even though the child may appear to have coped, these taught emotions often erupt as anger, aggression, frustration, or loneliness.

3. At times, some children put all their thoughts and feelings in the emotional suitcase, and slam it shut. Although, later,that suitcase has to be reopened. When this happens, the suit case explodes and all the feelings tumble out. Children may even attempt to lock the suit case trying to never allow themselves to feel the grief but that baggage becomes heavier as they grow older and they cannot deal with all the emotional aspects of their lives. (Gaffney, 1988).

When we think of grief and loss, the first thought is usually that of death and the loss of loved ones. This is only a very small part of grief and loss. As children are developing, grief and loss are part of their everyday lives. Sometimes even caregivers are unaware. Children read and hear stories or watch television programs about loss. For example, children experience loss when they; change schools, move to new homes, gain new siblings, lose precious possessions, are affected by the loss of personal status, lose pets, experience the death of a sibling, experience the death of a parent or grandparent, or, in today's society, even change parents. To help them cope with these changes we need to understand the grief process ourselves.

What Is Grief?

Grief is the psychological, social, and physical reaction to one's perception of loss. This definition has five important implications that provide essential information about grief.

1. Grief is experienced psychologically (through feeling, thoughts, and attitudes), socially (through behavior toward others), and physically (through health and bodily symptoms).

2. Grief is a continuous development, involving many changes over time. It will come and go and appear different at different times.

3. Grief is a natural, expectable reaction. The absence of grief is abnormal in most cases.

4. Grief is the reaction to all kinds of losses, not just death.

5. Grief is based on the individual's perception of the loss. It is not necessary that the loss be recognized or validated by others for an individual to experience grief. (Rando, 1988).

What Are Losses?

Losses may be either physical or symbolic.

1. Physical losses are tangible. Examples of physical losses are losing a parent due to death, having a special bike stolen, or losing a house to fire or natural disaster.

2. Symbolic losses are often not identified as losses. These are psychological in nature and are related to the psychological aspects of an individual's social interactions. These are abstract. These might include losing social status, losing a friend due to an argument or a move, or dealing with the effects of a divorce.

Loss always results in deprivation of some kind. Some like the theft of a bike or the loss of a parent are easily recognized. Some losses are less clearly recognized and do not result from negative events. Change itself always involves a loss. It upsets the status quo of things. Whether a change is positive or negative, there is always some loss and grief associated with it.

As we think about our lives, the most difficult times have involved a loss of some kind, whether physical or symbolic. Some people falsely believe they have never grieved because they have never experienced the death of a loved one. All of us grieve thousands of times over in our lifetime. Grief is the natural reaction to loss and loss is part of the natural process of our existence. It is obvious that some losses will not produce the same amount of grief as the loss of a loved one. However, the very same process of grief that causes the sadness of a child whose best friend refuses to play with him/her, also causes the full-blown grief response of the man whose wife was killed in an accident. (Rando, 1998).

What Are Grief Responses?

Grief is work. One must actively do things and develop thought patterns to resolve grief.

Grief responses to death fall into several stages.

1. In the avoidance stage the individual exhibits shock, denial, or disbelief.

2. In the anger or confrontational stage the individual is very emotional and seems to repeatedly learn that a loved one is dead. Grief is felt more intently.

3. In the bargaining stage, the individual might begin thinking with the phrase, "If only". For the child, it might be, "I'll learn my multiplication tables if only Grandpa would come back."

4. In the depression stage one realizes that denial, anger, and bargaining fail to make the situation better. The reality of death is acknowledged.

5. In the re-establishment stage, the individual gradually feels a decline in the acute grief and begins an emotional reentry into the everyday world.

These phases are broad and general. Individuals usually move back and forth between the stages. The length of the grieving process differs from individual to individual. (Seibert, Drolet, and Fetro, 1993).

How Grief Affects Individuals

Just as the length of the grieving process differs with individuals, so does the effects of grief. Grief affects people psychologically, socially, and physically.

Those working with children should be aware of these things:

1. Grief may be evidenced as anxiety. A child may become overly anxious about normal activities or fearful of new and old surroundings. When comforting a grieving child, we should not say, "Grandpa is asleep and will sleep forever."A statement like this may lead the child to say, "I don't want to go to sleep tonight."

2. Anger and guilt is another evidence of grief. Individuals may become angry at the person or feel guilty that they did not do what they feel they should have done for the deceased person.

3. Loss of faith and anger at God is often evidenced. A child may especially feel slighted. We may say, "Grandpa was so good that God wanted him to live with him forever and ever." The child may think, "Well, I loved him, too. I want him with me. If God takes those that are good, I want to stay here so I'll be bad."

4. Depression is another response to grief. It is especially important that we recognize the signs of depression in children. Associated with the state of depression, the child may suffer confusion, a lack of ability to concentrate, physical complaints, problems sleeping, or sleeping too much, crying at inappropriate times, suffer withdrawal from friends, or decreased socialization. He/she may choose to escape into books or television. Associated with depression may be suicidal thoughts. Although these thoughts are not usually acted upon, children whom we suspect are suffering the effects of depression should be evaluated by a qualified medical professional. (Beckman, 1990).

Stages of Understanding Grief and Loss for Children

There are predictable developmental stages of understanding for children. The first of these is the concrete or physical stage. He/she must be able to see or touch to understand. As the child develops, he/she learns to reason and to think about things that cannot be touched. At this time he/she is entering into the abstract developmental stage. Each stage of understanding must be completely explored before the child moves to the next stage. This is true in all learning including how to deal with grief and loss.

Stage One: Under Three Years of Age

Because of limited verbal communication, this age group is difficult to study. Due to different abilities, different experiences, and different degrees of adult guidance, some two year olds may understand death and react to it. A bright two year old may exhibit changes in behavior when someone or something important is removed from his/her life. This leads researchers to believe that this age child may understand far more than he/she is able to verbalize.

Stage Two: Ages Three Through Five

At this stage a child is unable to see death as final. It is viewed as temporary. The world of this age child focuses around himself/herself (egocenticism). Unless personally affected by a death or loss, a child may accept the words but the words have no meaning for him/her. Even when the child is directly affected by a death or loss, due to this self-centered stage, he/she may believe the death or loss to be due to his/her own actions. He/she needs assurance that this is not true. This stage child also has the characteristic of animism in which he/she believes inanimate objects are alive. The child cannot understand the differences between life and death. He/she believes in magical thinking. An intelligent child may use magical thinking powers as a fix-it. He/she may say, "If I give Mom a four leaf clover, she will not be sick anymore." This helps the child see grief or loss as reversible and avoidable.

Stage Three: Ages Six to Eight

In this stage a child is learning to see death as final and the end for all living things, except himself/herself. The child experiences much personal conflict and is very interested in the details of death. He/she questions the cause of the death or loss and begins to question what happens after death.

Stage Four: Ages Nine and Up

It is in this stage that a child usually reaches an adult-like understanding of death. He/she understands that death is final, inevitable, and personal. He/she understands the medical terms of death and can understand that memories keep a loved one alive or that someone was returned to the earth. A child in this age group, even though he/she may have the mental abilities to understand, may lack coping skills. He/she needs much emotional support at a time of loss or grief. (Seibert, Drolet, Fetro, 1993).

Support Systems for Children

It is of great importance that as children experience grief and loss the adults in their lives act as their support systems. The grief process for children may actually be much worse than for adults due to their understanding and reasoning abilities. The teachers of these children may be their strongest support and their best line of defense because they see them every day in a consistent, structured environment. Often children say or do things in school that they would not say or do at home. Young children take comfort in hearing questions and comments from their peers. As they are allowed to talk and later draw pictures, their artwork may provide insight into their perception of the loss. (Gaffney, 1988).

Compassion

Just as grief and loss must be dealt with for children to develop healthy character, it is equally important that children learn to show compassion towards others. When children show compassion, they identify with the emotions of others and respond by being kind to others, helping those in need, and doing good deeds without expecting anything in return.

We must teach children to be the "shoulder to cry on" when a friend is sad. We must teach children to be kind to strangers in need of food, clothing, shelter, or medical attention. We must teach children that being compassionate is not always easy because it often means putting others and their needs ahead of our own.

Conclusion

Children learn about grief and loss in small steps as their experiences and abilities grow with their ability to read. As educators and parents, we must discover what they already know and what they are capable of understanding. It is not necessary that we know all the answers but we must demonstrate a willingness to admit that our answers are not always right, but we can be available to help children search for answers.

What Do Children Need to Know About Grief and Loss?

☞ **They must know the facts.**
☞ **They must share feelings.**
☞ **They must share beliefs.**
☞ **They must learn coping skills.**

Half-truths and false information lead to fear and misunderstandings. Children, with the help of honest adults, can benefit from life's experiences. Otherwise they may make up their own accounts of the truth. They must be given accurate information that answers their questions in a manner that they can easily understand according to their own level of personal development. (Seibert, Drolet, Fetro, 1993).

Moving

I Like It Here Just Fine

Objectives

1. To help children understand that it is sometimes necessary for a family to relocate.

2. To help the children understand that moving to a new house and neighborhood may be both traumatic and rewarding.

3. To help children understand the importance of maintaining old and developing new friendships.

4. To help children develop compassion toward a new classmate or person in the neighborhood.

5. To help children learn ways to make new friends.

Overview

Trace and Cameron are two young next door neighbors. Their summer days are spent together playing in the backyard. Both are very athletically inclined and enjoy racing, swinging, and biking. They pride themselves on being the fastest boys in town and on being a team. Then one day Trace's father announces that they will be moving to a new, bigger home. Trace is very insecure about the move. Then he meets his new neighbor Dylan Sands. Dylan, too, likes to race, swing, and bike and describes himself as the fastest boy in town.

Discussion Questions

1. How did Trace feel at the beginning of the story? How did he feel at the end of the story?
2. Describe the friendship of Trace and Cameron. What made them such good friends?
3. Why do you think it is sometimes hard to move?
4. What makes a neighborhood a good place to live?
5. What would you say to a friend who is sad because he/she is moving?

Suggested Activities

1. Things We Do Role Play
As a group, discuss the things that best friends do for each other. Make a list of the suggested things. Have the students role play these things and tell why each is acceptable. Focus on how these things help our friends.

2. Things We Never Do Role Play
As a group make a list of things best friends would never do to each other. Have the students role play these things and tell why each would be unacceptable behavior. Focus on how these things hurt others.

3. Feelings Change
Discuss Trace's feelings at the beginning, middle, and end of the story. Lead the students to discover how his feelings changed and what caused the change in his feelings.

4. Reassurance Letters
Invite the students to write letters to Trace explaining to him why he is going to like the new house.

5. Happy Letters
Have the students pretend to be Trace. Have them write letters to Cameron telling all about the new house and his new friend Dylan Sands.

6. Invitations
Have the students pretend to be Trace. Have them write an invitation inviting Cameron to their birthday party. Have them decorate the outside of the invitation.

7. Moving Day
Have the students write a story entitled *Moving Day* . When the stories are complete, allow the students to make the stories into books and illustrate them. These might include packing boxes, packing the truck, leaving the old house, or saying goodbye to old friends. Have them share the books with the class or with other classes. Students could also work in teams to complete this activity.

8. Venn Diagrams
As a group, complete a venn diagram contrasting Trace's feelings at the time he moved and after being settled in his new house. Also, you could include a diagram comparing the things he does in both places.

9. Good Is Bad
Discuss with the students that often when we think something like a move is terrible it turns out good. Also, when we think something is very good, it can turn out very bad. This game focuses on some bad qualities of some very nice things. No materials are required. There is no special room arrangement. Allow about twenty-five minutes for playing time. The game is as follows:

A. Ask everyone to think about a favorite thing. It can be a toy or object, a place, or a person.

B. Have each person think about the bad qualities of their favorite thing. What are the things it cannot do? What are the ways it may be harmful.

C. Give each child an opportunity to describe a favorite thing in unfavorable terms with out telling what the thing is. Encourage them to make their thing sound as awful as they can without lying. For example: If the favorite thing is a balloon, a player may say,"You can't sit on it. You have to be careful or it will explode. It doesn't last long. It can't be stored with straight pins."

D. Allow the students to guess what his/her favorite object is. If all the players are stumped, and if the speaker has run out of bad things to say, suggest giving a good clue. The first person to guess what it is goes next to describe his/her favorite object.

10. Estimation

Have the students estimate how many of their classmates have moved. Have them write their estimation down. Then with the students' help, make a list of the ones who have moved and those who have not moved. Use tally marks to record that number. Find the student who guessed most accurately.

11. Word Problem Stories

Make a list with the students' help of the students who have moved and those who have not moved. Have the students use the totals to write math stories for addition and subtraction. Have them solve their problems or give them to a friend to solve.

12. Moving Around the Class

Many times children in the classroom tend to play and interact with the same students. This activity will help them to become better acquainted with other students in the class. Inform the students that for this activity they will move quietly around the room and find other classmates who are like them in some ways. To find how they are alike, they will find the answers to some questions. Have them write the names of the people who are like them. The teacher will have prepared prior to class time these directions:

- Find someone who has a birthday in the same month as your birthday.
- Find someone who has the same number of brothers and sisters as you.
- Find someone who plays on a soccer team.
- Find someone who has the same color of eyes as you.
- Find someone who is the only child in his/her family.
- Find someone who takes martial arts.
- Find someone who plays on a baseball or softball team.
- Find someone who likes your favorite television show.

- Find someone who has an older brother or sister.
- Find someone who has a baby in their house.

Tell the students they will have fifteen minutes to find their answers. Use a timer to keep time. When the time is up, ask everyone to come into a circle on the floor. If anybody did not find all the answers on his/her sheet, allow the group to help him/her. First, ask the students what they learned from this activity. Then explain to the students that we all know each other but we still found out new things about our friends. When we move, we will find people that are like us in many ways, also. Just as it took us a little time to find the people in our class for our answers, it may take a little time to find our new friends.

13. Drawing Your Home

Give each child a twelve by eighteen inch piece of manila art paper. Have them fold the paper into four equal parts and number the parts 1, 2, 3, and 4. In box 1 have them draw their home. In box 2 have them draw their best friend's home. In box 3 have them draw their grandmother's home. In box 4 have them draw the home of their dreams. Have them color the houses. Display the homes and discuss the differences and likeness of the homes. Help them realize that just as we are all different, so are our homes and that no matter what kind of home you live in, it is often sad when you have to move away.

14. Different Homes

Brainstorm with the class the different kinds of homes in which people live. Encourage them to mention individual houses, duplexes, apartments, housing projects, houseboats, cars, shelters, etc.

Follow-up Tips For Parent(s)

Moving can be an emotionally difficult time for a child, especially if he/she has developed good relationships in the neighborhood. If you are contemplating a move, you might use this book to consider these things:

1. Talk about the relationship of Cameron and Trace in the story. Stress that the friendship did not end because of the move.

2. Allow your child to become acquainted with the idea of moving as soon as possible.

3. Allow the child to make decisions about his/her room and other areas of the house, if possible.

4. Help the child develop new relationships in the new neighborhood, school, or church/synagogue/temple as soon as possible.

5. Help the child to understand that making new friends can lead him/her to new experiences like meeting Dylan introduced Trace to fishing.

Adoption

I Grew In Mommy's Heart

Objectives

1. To allow children to discuss the process of adoption.

2. To help children understand that birth parents often make great sacrifices when placing a child for adoption.

3. To develop the idea that it takes more than the birthing process to become good parents.

4. To lead children to conclude that all children are special.

Overview

Hannah, the main character in this story, is adopted. She has a very close, loving relationship with her adopted parents. As the story unfolds, she questions her father about the new baby that is soon to be adopted into the family. She asks questions about her own birth mother. Her father answers explaining that her birth mother had to love her dearly to give her up so she could have a better life. He reinforces the idea that a real mother takes care of and loves her child and that just birthing a child does not make one a real mother. As the story ends, a call is received from the adoption agency to come for as new little brother.

Discussion Questions

1. What words would you use to describe Hannah's father?

2. What does it mean to be adopted?

3. Why is an adopted child special? Why is a natural birth child special?

4. Why do you think Hannah had all those questions for her dad?

5. How do you feel about someone who would give their child up for adoption? How do you think that person must feel?

Suggested Activities

1. **Introduction and Sharing of Book**
   Talk about the meaning of birth parents, natural parents, and adopted parents. Read the book aloud or have students read silently.

2. **What Parents Do**
   Instruct half of the group, working individually, to think of things adopted children do with their adopted parents and make a list of these things. Instruct the other half of the group, working individually, to think of things natural children do with their natural parents. Make a list of these things. When ample time has been allotted, bring both groups together and discuss the things they have written. Lead them to discover that adoptive families and natural families do the same things together.

3. **Nursery Design**
   Have the students draw and color the nursery for Hannah's new brother. Discuss how the family prepares for a new baby the same way a natural mother and father prepare for a new baby.

4. Why Parents Give Their Babies Up

Lead the class in a discussion of the reasons some parents must give their children up for adoption.

5. Family Portrait

Have the students draw a portrait of Hannah's new brother or of the entire family including the new brother.

6. The Adopted Child

Have the students write stories about a child who was adopted and the feelings of that child. Allow them to share the stories and discuss the feelings of the child in the different stories.

7. The Birth Mother

Have the students write stories about the birth mother who chose to give her child up for adoption. Have the students share these stories and discuss the feelings of the birth mother.

8. Meet the New Parents

Have the students write stories about the adoptive parents and their feelings. Share the stories and discuss their feelings.

9. Letter Writing

Have the students pretend to be the adopted child. Have them write letters to the adopted parents and/or the birth mother.

10. *I Am Special* Sing-a-Long

Write the words to this song on poster paper. After singing, help the students add additional verses. (Sung to Twinkle, Twinkle, Little Star see next page).

I am special, you can see.
Mom and Dad have chosen me
To share their house and all their love
They said I came from heaven above.

I am special, you can see.
Mom and Dad adopted me.

11. Am I Special?

Write the words to this song on poster paper. After learning these verses, allow the students to help add additional verses. (Sung to the tune of "Are You Sleeping?")

Am I special? Am I special?
Yes Sirree! Yes Sirree!
There's no other like me, There's no other like me,
And won't ever be, and won't ever be.

God made my eyes. God made my eyes
For me to see, for me to see
All of His great world, all of His great world
the land and the sea, the land and the sea.

12. Culture Collages

Point out that most families are alike in some ways and yet different in other ways. Provide old magazines. Allow the students to look through the magazines to find pictures of families. Cut these out and make a family collage. When the collages are finished, allow time for each child to share his/her collage and point out how the families are alike and how they are different. Be sure to point out that all children do not have the same physical characteristics of their parents.

13. *I Am Special* Necklaces

Give each child a diamond shaped piece of construction paper that measures about five inches by five inches. Instruct them to write sentences or draw pictures on the diamond that tell what makes them special. Encourage them to fill the necklace and then decorate it. Punch a hole in the top of the diamond and thread a length of yarn through the hole. Allow the students to wear their necklaces.

14. What's In A Name?

Use the names of various students in the classroom and write acrostic poems with each line beginning with a letter of the child's name.

An example is as follows:

J - Join us on the playground!

O - Oh, we will have such fun!

H - Help us find new games to play

N - Next we'll jump and hop and run.

15. Yards of Smiles

Emphasize the uniqueness of each child by inviting them to enter your smile contest. Divide the class into teams of two. Give each pair of students a tape measure. Ask each partner to put on his/her biggest smile. Each student measures the smile of his/her partner and records the measurement on a prepared poster. Give a small prize to the boy and girl with the biggest smile. (This can be extended to include measuring around the wrist, the head, ankle, length of arm, etc.).

Follow-up Tips For Parent(s)

This book is for the special children who have been adopted. Adopted children often do have questions about their birth parents. Psychologists tell us that the best answers to their questions are the truthful answers. Always encourage the child to express and not suppress these questions. Answer the questions in a manner age appropriate for your child, reassuring him/her of their specialness and your love for him/her. (Salk, 1979).

1. Talk about how the family worked together to accomplish tasks.

2. Talk about the ways the family showed love for Hannah.

House Fire

Ashes and More Ashes

Objectives

1. To stress that the loss of personal possessions can cause much hardship and grief.

2. To help children understand that house fires affect all economic levels of people.

3. To encourage the use of home fire safety.

4. To discover the importance of ways to show compassion toward others who may have lost their homes due to a fire.

Overview

The family awakens to a beautiful, snowy Saturday. After a day filled with outdoor fun, the last of the clothes are peeled off and laid on the fireplace to dry. While the family is sleeping, the clothes on the fireplace catch fire and the entire house is soon engulfed in flames. The family safely flees the house saving only their lives. Neighbors and friends come to the rescue supplying personal needs. Fellow church members pool their efforts and resources to rebuild the house for the family.

Discussion Questions

1. How did the story begin for Austin and Hunter?

2. Use your own words to tell how Austin and Hunter felt at the end of the day after playing in the snow?

3. What happened to wake them in the night? How do you think they felt?

4. What thoughts and feelings do you think Austin and Hunter had the morning after the fire?

5. Make a list of all the words you can think of to describe their neighbors.

Suggested Activities

1. **Adult Feelings**
   After sharing the book, discuss the feelings of Mom and Grandpa at the beginning, the middle, and the end of the story. Ask the children if it is acceptable for adults to cry. Have them express why they feel as they do. Be sure to help them understand that tears can be a way to express their sadness. Ask how were the adults' feelings different from the feelings of the children?

2. **Before and After Pictures**
   Divide the class into three work groups. Assign one group of students to draw pictures of the house prior to the fire. Have one group of students draw pictures of the house after the fire. Have one group of students draw pictures of the new house. Display these in the classroom.

3. **Brainstorming Burned Items**
   Lead the students in brainstorming a list of things destroyed by the fire. Then categorize these things into groups such as clothing, toys, food items, furniture, linens, important papers, pictures, etc. Help the students to understand the devastation of a house fire. Ask students what possessions they would miss most.

4. **Working Together Sing-a-Long**

Discuss with the children the importance of the neighbors working together to rebuild the house. Ask them how the neighbors learned to work with others. Stress that as classmates they often work together to complete tasks just as the neighbors worked on the house. Have the song written on a chart so the students can see and read the words. Then have the students sing together the song. It is sung to the tune of "If You're Happy and You Know It."

Helping Out

If your neighbor has a problem, help him out.
If your neighbor has a problem, help him out.
If your neighbor has a problem, help him out, you'll both feel better.
If your neighbor has a problem help him out.

If your friend needs a hug, give him one.
If your friend needs a hug, give him one.
If your friend needs a hug, give him one, and say I love you.
If your friend needs a hug give him one.

Allow the children to help add additional verses to the song.

5. **Sad and Happy Feelings**

Have each student make a sad and smiley face. Allow them to secure them to popsicle sticks. Have prepared sentence strips of these statements about the story. As you hold up and read a sentence strip, have the students show the smiley face for a happy feeling or the sad face for an unhappy feeling to match the feeling that the action in the sentence caused.

A. Austin said, "It's snowing again. I don't want it to ever snow again."
B. Austin and Hunter make snow angels.
C. Mother fixed grits, bacon, and eggs for breakfast.
D. There was nothing left but smoke where their house stood.
E. They drank delicious hot chocolate together and warmed by the fire.
F. Grandpa said, "We have nothing left."

G. The children saw tears in the eyes of Mom and Grandpa.

H. The neighbors brought toys and furniture for the family.

I. Mom lay the wet clothes by the fire to dry.

J. Men and women from the church work to rebuild the family's little yellow house.

After the students make each response, allow them to share the reasons they chose a sad or smiley face for their answer.

6. Fire Safety Unit

Develop a unit of study on fire safety. Included in this study should be the following:

A. Stress the importance of working fire alarms.

B. Assign a home fire safety check of the storage areas for combustible materials. Have the students encourage their parents to rid their homes of these.

C. Stress the importance of keeping papers, clothing, furniture, and curtains, ect. away from portable heaters.

D. Assign each child to develop a map of his/her home and a fire escape route with his/her family.

E. Stress the importance of keeping matches and lighters away from small children.

F. Help each child learn his/her full name, parents' full names, address, and home phone number. Have them practice calling 911 and giving this information.

G. Teach the children to stop, drop, and roll, in the event of a clothing fire.

H. Show the children how to crawl on the floor if the room should be filled with smoke.

I. Plan a visit to the local fire department, or have them visit your school.

7. Fire Safety Song

To reinforce the concepts taught in the fire safety unit, write the following song on chart paper and help the students to learn it. It is sung to the tune of "London Bridge".

Fire Safety

Fire can burn up all your things,
All your things, all your things,
Fire can burn up all your things
And send them up in smoke.

Fire can burn up books and toys,
Books and toys, books and toys,
Fire can burn up books and toys,
And we'll have nothing left.

Fire can burn our walls and floor,
Walls and floor, walls and floor,
Fire can burn our walls and floor,
And also burn our roof.

We can learn to all be safe,
All be safe, all be safe,
We can learn to all be safe,
If we follow safety rules.

Never play with matches and lighters,
Matches and lighters, matches and lighters,
Never play with matches and lighters,
Each can start a fire.

Check the fire alarm at home,
Alarm at home, alarm at home,
Check the fire alarm at home,
It can save your life.

Learn to stop and drop and roll,
Drop and roll, drop and roll,
Learn to stop and drop and roll,
If your clothes catch fire.

Yes, fire can burn up all your things,
All your things, all your things,
Fire can burn up all your things,
That's why we learn fire safety.

8. Help Your Neighbor

Write the letter found below, on chart paper and post it in the classroom. Allow the students to read the letter. Ask each student to answer the letter telling why he/she would be a good choice.

> Dear Students,
>
> I am looking for a student who can be responsible for checking my house to see if my family and I are practicing fire safety. Please write me a letter telling me why you are the right person for the job and how you will do this task.
> > Love,
> > Your Teacher

When the students have finished their letters, allow them to share their writing with the class.

9. Brain Teasing Math

For math use word problems like the following to correlate with the theme of fire.

A. The family went to bed at 9:00pm. They were awakened at 12:00am by the fire alarm. How long had they been sleeping?

B. The class collected toys for the boys in the story. They brought 10 toy trucks, 2 fire trucks, 1 jeep, 1 toy barn, and 3 tractors. How many toys were brought in all?

C. To help the family who lost it's house in the fire, Mrs. Brown's class collected 46 pennies, 65 dimes, 15 nickels, and 10 quarters for them. How much money did they collect in all? (You may use the calculator.)

D. The class brought food for the family. They brought 7 cans of tomato soup, 5 cans of green beans, 10 cans of peas, 2 cans of potato soup, 2 boxes of crackers, and 2 jars of peanut butter. Make a graph of the things they brought.

E. Mrs. Jones has 27 children in her class. Each child was asked to bring 2 cans of food for the family. If every child brings his/her cans, how many cans will they bring in all?

10. Climb to Safety

Prepare a worksheet that has a ladder with eight or ten steps. Instruct the students to think of one favorite thing for each step of the ladder that a fire would destroy if their house burned. Have them write one thing on each step of the ladder.

11. Fire Safety Flowers

Prepare patterns for flower petals. Have available small paper plates, green and yellow construction paper, glue, pencils and crayons, and scissors. Allow each child to make eight yellow petals using the petal patterns and cut them out. Give each child a paper plate and have them write "Fire Safety" on it. On each petal have them write one fire safety rule. Display the fire safety flowers around the room.

12. Fire Reporters

Have the students become reporters and write an article for the newspaper about the fire.

13. Book Making

Divide the class into work teams of three or four students. Have each group pretend to be one of the family members in the story. Have them write a story about the fire from the perspective of that family member. After the stories are complete, have the students work in teams to create a book about the fire. The students could also develop a book for children who have experienced a fire. In this they could include activities that offer hope and understanding.

14. Thanking Friends

Have the students pretend to be either the grandpa or mother in the story. Have them make thank you cards and write notes in them thanking the neighbors for their help.

15. Fire Safety Rule Book

Ask the class to make a book of fire safety rules. Have them illustrate it and then display it. Or the class could do a presentation for younger students.

16. Poetry Writing

- Make a classroom poster poem entitled PREVENTING FIRES.
- Lead the students in writing an acrostic poem about fire prevention.

P - *Place things far away from flames.*
R - *Replace fire alarm batteries.*
E -
V -
E -
N -
T -
I -
O -
N -

17. Community Compassion

If a family within the school's community has had their home destroyed by fire, organize a class-wide or school-wide drive for food and clothing. First, check the items needed with the family. Then make a prepared list of these things to send home with the students. Have the students make posters to put at various places in the school telling needed items, the day for drop off, and the drop-off site. Allow the students to help sort the items if necessary. Have parent volunteers deliver the collected goods to the needy family. After the drive is complete talk with the students about their feelings as they helped others.

18. Fire Safety Puzzle

Write sentences about fire safety or showing compassion to others who have had a fire on sentence strips. Cut each sentence apart and place it in a plastic bag. (I find it helpful to number each cut piece to correspond with the number on a bag for easier sorting if the words should become mixed up.) Allow the students to put the words back together into sentences and read the sentences. Do several of these such as:

- Matches belong away from children.
- Keep clothes away from heaters.
- If your clothes are on fire, stop, drop, and roll.

- In an emergency dial 911.
- We feel good when we help others.
- Fire can destroy our whole house.

Follow-up Tips For Parent(s)

The loss of personal items in a fire brings emotions of grief. In this story the family lost not only the house structure but all personal belongings. Even though there was no loss of life, there was much grief and much healing to be done.

1. Talk to your child about the dangers of fire.

2. Develop with your child an evacuation route from your house to be used in the event of a fire and set an outside meeting place for all family members.

3. Teach your child to dial 911 and stress the importance of using it only in emergencies. Make sure your child can give the full name of his/her parents, the home street address, and the home telephone number.

4. Talk about the cooperation of the neighbors as they worked to provide the necessities for the fire victims. Stress the importance of their compassion toward the family.

New Baby

Story Four
Take Her Back

Objectives

1. To discuss the feelings of older siblings when a new baby is born.

2. To help older siblings understand that sometimes the anticipation of a new baby is more exciting than the reality of its arrival.

3. To encourage older children who are feeling neglected by helping them realize that babies demand much attention and that it is okay to feel and express jealousy toward a new baby.

4. To guide the children to discover acceptable ways to gain attention and become more accepting of the new arrival.

Overview

Joshua has a very happy life at home with his parents and younger brother. One morning he announces to his preschool class that his mother is having a new baby and that his mom said it was a very pleasant surprise. However, when the new baby arrives, it does not prove to be the promised pleasant surprise. Instead he feels very alone and very neglected until his mom finds a way to spend quality time with him.

Discussion Questions

1. What was the reason Joshua did not want to go to the hospital to get his mom?

2. Do you think Joshua would really like to give the new baby away?

3. Why do you think Josh's mom said she needed some time off, too?

4. Do you have a new baby at your house? If so, what are some good things about having a new baby? Are there any bad things about having a new baby?

5. How can parents help the older children learn to better adjust to a new baby?

Suggested Activities

1. **Exploring Jealousy**
   Have the students discuss the story and help them conclude that Joshua was jealous of the new baby. Have them recall ways that the mother and father in the story tried to help the older children adjust to the new baby. Ask if any of them were ever jealous of a sibling. Explain that it is normal to feel jealous.

2. **Plan for the Baby**
   Have the students pretend that a new baby is expected in their families. Have them help to make a list of things that will be needed. As each item is named, write it on the chalkboard or poster board. Then help the students categorize the items as:
   A. Bath items
   B. Food Items
   C. Clothing Items
   D. Toys

3. **Nursery Design Contest**
   Divide the class into teams with four members in each team. Assign each team to design and color a nursery for the new baby. After all the nurseries are complete, invite another

class to look at the nurseries and vote by secret ballot for the one they think is best. Reward each participant in the design contest.

4. Baby Acrostic Antics

Have each child write the letters of one of the words down the side of a sheet of paper. They may choose babies, sisters, or brothers. They are to think of words or phrases that describe their word that begins with each letter of the word. Have the children take turns sharing their acoustics with the group and explaining why they chose the words they chose. For example:

- Burp
- Always wet
- Bump their noses
- Inch across the floor
- Eat baby food
- Sit in high chairs

5. Love Letters

Have the students pretend to be Joshua. Have them write love letters to their parents telling how they love them and how they feel about the new baby. Encourage them to tell all the pleasant things as well as the unpleasant things associated with the new baby.

6. Mads/Sads/Scares/Glads

For the child who perceives that he/she has lost his/her position in the family, set aside fifteen minutes per day. Have the child list all the things that bother him/her since the new baby's arrival. This is to be done only during the allotted time so it does not dominate his/her thinking. For a younger child, he/she might be encouraged to draw pictures to express his/her feelings in each category. Then talk with the child about his/her feelings and discuss ways he/she can still get his/her needs met. Examples of how they may feel are:

A. I am mad you came to our house.
B. I am frustrated you cry so much.
C. I am upset Mommy holds you so much.
D. I am sad that Daddy can't play with me as much.

Help them re-phrase these statements to the following:

    A. I am still very important to my parents.
    B. When you cry I can help you feel safe.
    C. I can help Mommy hold you and feed you.
    D. Even though Daddy needs to spend time with you, he and I can still have our special time.

7. Welcome Home Cards

Have the students design welcome home cards for mother and the new baby. After the designs are complete, have the students write a message to the mother telling her how glad they are to have them at home.

8. Create Affirmations

To help a child who feels lonely, have him/her write the same affirmation about himself/herself 10 to 25 times skipping lines on his paper. The number of times it is written would vary by the age of the child. Under each affirmation, have him/her write a negative discount that pops into his/her mind. Have the child keep going until the negative self-talk ends. Then have him/her make a new affirmation from the discounts that have been written. Keep doing this for several days. Examples:

    A. I am not wanted or loved.
       I am wanted and loveable.
    B. Mom doesn't want me any more.
       Mom wants me and loves me, too.
    C. Dad doesn't want me.
       Dad wants me and loves me like always.

New Affirmation: My Mom and Dad want me and love me because I am special and loveable.

    A. Mother loves the baby more.
       She cooks my food, too.
    B. Mother loves the baby more.
       She washes my clothes, too.

C. Mother loves the baby more.
   She reads my books to me.

New affirmation: Mother loves me as much as the baby but she can't do things for herself.

9. **You're A Parent**

To emphasize the amount of time required with a new baby provide each student with a worksheet that says, "Congratulations! You are a new parent." Have each child make a schedule for his/her baby. Inform him/her that he/she is to allow time to do the housework, cook the meals, do the laundry, bathe the baby, feed the baby, and care for the two other children. After the schedules are made, have the student compare his/her schedule with the ones of friends. Ask if any student had difficulty finding enough time in his/her day to do all the required things. If so, what does this tell you about your parents?

10. **Create Birth Announcements**

Help the children to make birth announcements for the new baby. Have them include the baby's name, parent's names, date of birth, weight, and length. Then have them sign the doctor's name.

11. **He/She's My Pleasant Surprise**

Have the students write a story about the new baby. Have them tell all about the baby...what it does, who it looks like, where it sleeps, how they feel about it.

12. **Find Someone Who**

To help students discover more about their classmates and themselves and to foster an appreciation of individual differences, play the game, "Find someone who". Give each child a pencil and an instruction sheet. Tell them to find one person in the class to fit each question and write that person's name on their paper by the statement.

   A. Has seen the Atlantic Ocean
   B. Has a big brother
   C. Plays the piano
   D. Likes to sing

E. Has a baby in their house
F. Can play soccer
G. Has a big sister
H. Plays T-Ball or baseball
 I. Takes dancing lessons
 J. Has had a part in a play

After the students are finished, ask if anyone discovered something about a friend that they did not know. Then ask, what makes each of us special? Lead the students to conclude that each of us is unique.

13. Child of the Year

Tell the students that each of them has just been chosen as a candidate for "Child of the Year." Tell them to write what they did or do to deserve the award.

14. Problem Solving

Have the students write how they might feel and their best solution for each situation.

1. Situation: Mom spends all her time with the new baby.

   Your feelings:_____

   Your solution:_____

2. Situation: Grandpa wants to take the baby home with him.

   Your feelings:_____

   Your solution:_____

3. Situation: Daddy was up most of the night when the baby cried. He is too tired to come to your game today.

   Your feelings:_____

   Your solution:_____

4. Situation: Mother has to cook dinner. She asks you to watch the baby. You want to play outside.

Your feelings:_____

Your solution:_____

15. **Baby of the Year Award**

Your family's new baby has just been named a candidate for the "Baby of the Year Award." If he/she wins, the entire family will be given a free vacation to any place in the entire United States. It is your job to convince the judges that your baby brother or sister deserves this award. Write a letter to the judges telling them why your baby brother or sister should be selected.

Follow-up Tips For Parent(s)

The birth of a new child is an emotional time for an older sibling. He/she is adjusting to shared time with the parents, exploring his/her own emotions, and discovering his/her new sibling. It is of utmost importance that each child be given adequate preparation for the birth and individual time after the birth (Bank and Kahn, 1982).

1. Ask your child why the father took time off work and why the grandparents came to help out?

2. Ask your child why Joshua had so many complaints about the new baby and Justin did not.

3. If you are expecting a new baby, allow your child to help plan for the baby.

4. If you are expecting a new baby, allow the older child to tour the hospital with you prior to the birth and explain that you will be away from him/her for a little while.

5. The new baby often receives many gifts. Purchase ahead a small present for the baby to give to the older siblings.

6. Involve the older siblings as much as possible in helping care for the infant. This allows them to feel needed and important.

Divorce

The Brown Suitcase

Objectives

1. To encourage children of separated or divorced parents to seek a support person or persons to share their feelings so healing can begin.

2. To help children understand that the divorce or separation is not their fault.

3. To enable the children to understand that separation or divorce does not end parental love for them.

4. To assist children of separation or divorce in discovering ways to cope with the changes and loss.

5. To encourage other students to practice compassion toward friends whose parents are separating or divorcing.

Overview

Whitney is given a brown suitcase as a Christmas present by her grandma. The suitcase is first used to pack the necessities for an overnight visit to her grandparents' home. Visits to their home help her to escape the frequent quarreling of her parents. One day she returns home from school to find her mom in tears and her dad packing. Her father moves to an apartment, her mother must go to work, and Whitney faces many adjustments. When she finally feels that her life is about normal again, her father introduces her to his special friend and her two children.

Discussion Questions

1. How do you think Whitney felt when her father moved to an apartment?

2. How did life change for Whitney when her father moved?

3. Do you have parents who do not live together? How does this make you feel?

4. If your parents do not live together, how do they help you to feel good about it? Make a list and share it with your parents.

5. Do you think life will ever be the same for Whitney?

6. How could you help a friend who is sad because his/her parents are getting a divorce?

Suggested Activities

1. Suitcases
A. Design: Give each child a 9 x 12 inch sheet of construction paper. Have him/her design and color his/her own suitcase and then cut it out. On the back of the suitcase have him/her brainstorm a list of things needed for a weekend trip. Then bring all the students together with their individual lists. Have the students use their lists to help make a master list of the items mentioned. Display the suitcases.

B. Suitcase Adventure: Have the students write make-believe stories about a special journey which they took with their suitcase. Tell them the suitcase can take them anywhere they wish to go. They are to write about the journey and what happened while they were there. Allow them to share the stories. Display the stories with the suitcases.

2. Why Parents Separate
Discuss the meaning of separation and divorce. Lead the students to discuss why it is sometimes necessary for parents to stop living together. Have them share the feelings that the children in the family might have when parents separate. Stress that all feelings are valid. Ask the children what would help a family get through such a difficult time.

Mention family counseling and a children's divorce group after they share their suggestions.

3. Picture Making

Have the students draw and color a picture of Whitney in the story. After the pictures are complete, display them. Talk about what Whitney is doing in the individual pictures and her feelings at that time. Ask if they think she was afraid at any time in the story? Ask what her parents did in the story to help her.

4. Diary Writing

Older children are often more inhibited from verbalizing their feelings and can be less threatened by diary writing. (Clapp, 1992). Ask the students to write their feelings in a diary. Emphasize that they do not have to share the diary unless they choose to do so and encourage them to write anything they are thinking.

5. Letter Writing

If a child does not see a parent or a parent is deceased, have him/her write letters to the absent parent expressing his/her feelings. Even if the letters are not mailed, writing the words helps the healing begin (Clapp, 1992).

6. Poetry Writing

With younger children, have them help to write the words for a classroom poem called "Families". Display the poem on a poster Older students could enjoy doing this activity alone or in small groups.

7. Keepsake Box

The divorce of parents causes grief in a child the same as death. It is the death of his/her family as he/she knows it. Allow the child to make a keepsake box in which special treasures of family relationships can be kept. This might include pictures, pamphlets from vacation, old greeting cards, or anything the child chooses to remember about the absent parent. Allow him/her to add to it until he/she no longer feels the necessity of doing so.

8. Scrapbooks

Invite the children to make family scrapbooks. The scrapbooks may include pictures, newspaper articles, cards, invitations, or other items of importance to the child. This will be a great record of family experiences that can be shared or enjoyed alone. Encourage him/her to add other items as they become available so that this becomes an ongoing activity.

9. Comic Strip Making

Put four or five blank squares on a piece of paper. Give each child one piece of paper. Instruct the child to draw himself in the comic strip talking to the parent who is absent from the household.

10. I Remember When

This simple game is good for younger children who are in grief. Have the children sit on the floor. Begin with an example such as this. "I remember when my mom would let me help her cook dinner." Allow each child to share a memory from his/her family.

11. Empty Chair

For the child who is suffering through a separation or divorce, place two chairs facing each other. If a photograph of the absent parent is available, put it on one of the chairs. Have the child sit in the other chair and talk to the absent parent's chair telling him or her all the things he/she wants to share-concerns or happy feelings. (This activity should be conducted by a counselor, psychologist, or someone with a counseling background.)

12. Puppets

This activity is for one child who is having difficulty adjusting to a parent being absent from the home. Give the child two brown paper lunch bags. Have him/her draw himself/herself on one and the absent parent on the other. Then have him/her put them on his/her hands and have the puppets start a conversation. Encourage him/her to express all his/her feelings to the parent puppet.

13. Friends Helping Friends

Give each child a brown paper lunch bag. Tell him/her to draw themselves on the bag. Divide the class into teams of four. Give a problem situation to one member of the group. Have him/her let his/her puppet read the problem to the other team members. They, in turn, use their puppets and offer suggestions to help the friend deal with the problem. Examples of problems might be:

- My mom and dad fuss all the time.
- My mom and dad said they are getting a divorce.
- I live with my mom. She works all the time. I get so lonely.
- My dad lives in another town. He tells me he will come see me but he sometimes forgets.

14. Make A List

This activity can be an ongoing activity that can be picked up and put down at a moment's notice. You need a large piece of paper and felt tipped markers. Choose a free wall and tape or tack up the paper so students can add to it during free times. Select a title such as one of these:

A. Make a list of things family members do for each other.

B. Make a list of things you would lose if your house burned.

C. Make a list of things you must do for a puppy.

15. Team Esteem

Children who are grieving through a separation and divorce often suffer from low self esteem. This activity is designed for compliments, compliments, compliments. Divide the class into teams with seven or eight to each team. Have each team make a circle. Give a team leader in each group a crushed paper ball. Tell him/her to toss the paper ball to another member of his/her team. As he/she tosses the ball, he/she is to give the other team member a compliment such as, "You are a great writer.", "You are a good listener.", or "I like how you draw". The player receiving the compliment tosses the ball to another team member and gives him/her a compliment. Continue the game until all members have given and received several compliments.

16. Support Available

Encourage the students to make a list of four people they could talk to about any problem they are having and check the appropriate box of a time they could talk to the person.

Name	Most of the Time	Some of the Time	Seldom
A. _____	_____	_____	_____
B. _____	_____	_____	_____
C. _____	_____	_____	_____
D. _____	_____	_____	_____

17. Relationships

Prepare the following worksheet. Have the students complete the worksheet to describe some of the people in their lives.

1. My favorite person is _____

   because_____.

2. My friend is _____

   because _____.

3. My parent(s) are _____

   because _____.

4. My teacher is _____

   because _____.

5. My grandparents are_____

   because _____.

Follow-up Tips For Parent(s)

To a child the divorce of his/her parents does not mean a second chance as it often does for the involved adults. It means the end of his/her family, support, stability, and security in an unpredictable world. The anxiety of the child is intense and can be eased if the child is given reassurance from both parents, (Clapp, 1992).

1. Talk to your child about the reasons for the separation of Whitney's parents.

2. Discuss Whitney's feelings and the feelings of her parents.

3. If you are a separated parent, ask your child to share his/her anxieties. Listen and make him/her aware that your love for him/her will not change. Assure the child that he/she is not responsible for the separation.

4. Encourage your child to be involved with other people and in outside activities to get his/her mind off the home situation.

5. If you are in the process of getting a divorce, and your child's school has a divorce group, talk with the counselor about getting him/her involved.

The Dinosaur Tamer

Dealing with a Bully

Objectives

1. To discuss the meaning of a bully.

2. To guide the children to understand that a bully often is very insecure.

3. To lead the children to discover appropriate methods of dealing with a bully.

4. To encourage the children to be accepting of and to make friends with new class members. Once they do, they may find things they have in common.

5. To help children understand that all people need to both show compassion to others and be shown compassion from others at different times in their lives.

Overview

Tyrone, a child small in stature, is new to the school. Andre, the largest boy in the class harasses him continuously. Tyrone does all he can to avoid him but Andre is always there. One morning Andre overhears Tyrone talking to another student. In the conversation, Tyrone makes the comment that he wishes dinosaurs were still alive because he would tame him one. From that day on, Andre never misses a chance to make fun of him and call him "The Dinosaur Tamer". One afternoon Tyrone and his grandmother go to the park to allow Tyrone to ride his bike. Andre is there on his bike, too. As Andre attempts to begin his harassing again, he has an accident and breaks his leg. Tyrone and his grandmother come to his rescue. After this, Andre realizes that Tyrone is a valuable friend.

Discussion Questions

1. Why did Tyrone have few friends at school?

2. How many friends do you think Andre had? Why do you feel this way?

3. If you had been Tyrone what would you have done when Andre called you names? Why?

4. Why do you think Andre called Tyrone names? How did this change later?

5. What words would you use to describe Andre? What words would you use to describe Tyrone?

6. Would you rather be like Andre or Tyrone? Why do you feel this way?

Suggested Activities

1. Identify Feelings

Have the students discuss the actions of the story characters. Have them discuss the reasons for their behaviors and the consequences of their behaviors.

2. Friendship Cards

Divide the class into pairs. Give each pair several index cards and drawing tools. Have the pairs work together to draw or describe situations that need compassionate responses such as a new child at school, a homeless person, someone who is very sad, someone who is very frightened, etc. When the cards are complete, have each pair show their cards and discuss possible responses to the situation. This should give many opportunities for the students to discuss many kinds of compassionate responses.

3. Thank You Notes

Have the students pretend to be Todd, the bully in the story. Ask them to write a thank you note to Tyrone for helping and being a friend.

4. Story Writing

Use story starters in the writing center or during whole group writing time. Encourage the students to express different ways they can show compassion toward others. The stories can be shared and then bound together to make a class book. Keep the book in the writing center so the students may read the stories of other students. Possible story starters are as follows:

- When someone is sick, I can...
- Once someone showed compassion to me by..
- Once I helped a friend by...
- Once upon a time, there was a boy/girl who was very kind. He/she always...
- When someone is sad, I can...
- When I am very sad, I hope someone will...
- When I am sick, I hope...

5. Share Good Wishes

Ask the students how they can show compassion to someone who is sick or disabled. Emphasize kindness and acceptance. Have the students make get well cards or cheer cards for patients in the local hospital, nursing home, hospice house, or children's home.

6. Role Play

Give the students various prompts of situations that need compassionate responses. Have selected children role play the situations. Possible scenarios might be:

- A new student
- A child who is sick
- An elderly grandparent
- A disabled child
- A young child who is absent from and missing his/her parents
- A friend who is having a bad day
- A friend who lost his/her favorite toy

7. All My Feelings Count

This activity is to help younger children understand the importance of feelings and to provide them practice at recognizing their feelings. You will need a group of pictures, music or smells that you think will arouse feelings in the children. You will also need to give each child three feeling cards. One card should have a smiling face, one should have a neutral face, and one should have a frowning face. Tell the children that you are going to find out how music, pictures, and smells make them feel. For each picture, piece of music, or smell that you present to the children, have them choose a card to tell how that item makes them feel. Remind them that we all have different feelings at different times. A feeling doesn't stay with you long. If you are feeling sad, sometimes a happy song will make you happy. Or, if you feel angry, a funny picture will make you laugh. Sometimes our feelings affect the way we act. Have the children think back over the things that made them happy, sad, or indifferent as you close the session. (Siebert, Drolet, Fetro, 1993)

8. Check the Newspaper

Have the students examine the newspaper for examples of people who are acting as bullies toward others. Ask them to cut out the pictures or articles and present them to the class. Then discuss the consequences of the bullying acts.

9. Billy the Bully

Help the class to write a poem entitled Billy the Bully. Include positive ways kids can deal with a bully. Display the poem in the classroom.

10. Bean Animal

Tell the children that animals have ways of dealing with their feelings of sad, mad, glad, or scared just as people do. Have them pretend to be a cat. Tell them that the big dog is coming up. Let them show what reaction the cat will have. Then, have them pretend to be a dog, rabbit, or turtle and have them act out situations that the animal might encounter. Then, ask why the animals react in this manner. Point out that the animals cannot talk. Help them to realize that unlike animals, people possess the ability to communicate with words and problem solve.

11. Cartoon Drawing

Give each child a piece of paper. Have them divide their paper into four equal parts and number each of the parts 1, 2, 3, 4. Have them draw a cartoon showing a bully in action and a good way of responding to the bully. Have them color the cartoon. Then allow time for them to share the cartoons. Display the cartoons in the room. If time allows, have the students role play a couple of the situations.

Follow-up Tips For Parent(s)

When children are dealing with new situations and crises, we find that they are resilient. There is much we can learn from them, but first, we have to listen. (Gaffney, 1988).

1. Ask your child why he/she thinks Tyrone never saw Andre with friends?

2. Ask your child how he/she thinks Tyrone must have felt being new in the school and neighborhood?

3. Discuss what Tyrone and Andre learned about each other later.

4. Talk with your child about the right ways to make new friends and the importance of listening to others.

5. Talk about the importance of helping other people and how it affects the person being helped and the person performing the good deed.

Foster Care

My New Foster Home

Objectives

1. To encourage children from abusive home situations to discuss their feelings with support persons.

2. To stress that abusive parents need professional help.

3. To emphasize that alcohol and drug abuse can lead to abusive situations.

4. To help children understand that when home situations are out of control, it is often best to remove the children until the parents receive the needed help.

5. To allow the children to discuss the meaning of foster care and foster parents.

6. To lead the children to an understanding of the feelings of foster children and to help them practice compassion toward them.

Overview

Savanna's father suffers from an addiction to alcohol. His addiction frequently causes a lack of money for food, rent, and school lunch money. Her mother attempts to protect her and her little brother Mark from him while he is in a drunken rage. Her intervention leads to his physical abuse of her. This is a pattern to which Savanna has become both accustomed and quite fearful. Her mother's late night screams arouse a neighbor who calls the police. This episode results in Savanna and Mark being placed in foster care for several months. The removal of his children from his home leads her father to examine his life and seek treatment for his addiction.

Discussion Questions

1. What is a foster home?

2. Why did Savanna and Mark have to go to a foster home?

3. Do you think the policemen should have taken Mark and Savanna from their parents? Why or why not?

4. What words would you use to tell about Savanna's feelings on the night she was taken from her home to the Adams' home?

5. What words would you use to describe Savanna's feelings on the morning she was returned to her home?

6. Have you ever known someone who drank too much alcohol? How did it make them act?

7. If a friend of yours is in a foster home, what could you do to help them?

Suggested Activities

1. Character Emotions

Savanna: Have the students identify the various emotions Savanna experienced in the story. Write these on the board as you discuss the causes of each emotion. Ask them how they would feel if they were in Savanna's place. Would they want their friends to know? Why or why not?

Savanna's Parents: Ask the students to think about the feelings of Savanna's mother and father at the beginning of the story. What did the parents feel when the children were taken away from them? How did the parents feel when the children were gone? How did they feel when the children were returned home?

The Policeman: Ask should the policemen have taken the children from their home? Why did they do it? What kind of men were the policemen? How do you know? How do you think the policemen felt to take the children away from their parents?

Mr. and Mrs. Adams: Have the students help you make a list of words to describe Mr. and Mrs. Adams. What did they do to help Mark and Savanna? Point out that the Adams' provided love and security for the children.

2. An Unexpected Journey

Have the students pretend to be Savanna. Have them write a story about the night they were taken from their home to the Adam's home.

3. Writing Home

Have the students pretend to be Savanna living with the Adam's family. Have them write a letter to their parents telling all about life at the Adam's house.

4. Book Writing

Divide the class into five groups. Have each group be responsible for making and illustrating a book about one of the characters from the book. (Savanna, Mark, Mom, Dad, Mr. and Mrs. Adams) Display the completed books after sharing them.

5. Alcohol Awareness

A. Help the students to make a definition of the word alcoholic. Write the definition in a prominent place.
B. Discuss the effects of alcohol abuse on the person who is abusing the alcohol.
C. Discuss the effects of alcohol abuse on the abuser's family.
D. Discuss that alcohol is an addictive drug that is legal and readily available.

6. Alcohol Collage

Provide old magazines. Allow the students to search through them for advertisements of alcoholic beverages and cut them out. Glue these onto poster board to make a class collage. Then discuss the people in the advertisements...their happiness, apparent wealth, and beautiful clothes. Ask the students why the advertisers show this image instead of situations like those in Savanna's home and people like Savanna's father. Discuss the reasons for this.

7. Alcohol Free Pledge
Invite the students to sign a pledge to remain drug and alcohol free. Display this in the classroom.

8. Thank You Notes
Have the students pretend to be Savanna. Have them design and write thank you notes to Mr. and Mrs. Adams.

9. Portrait Making
Have the students draw and color a picture of Savanna's family.

10. Support Pennants
Have the students design and color banners to help themselves remember when tempted to try alcohol or other drugs to make the right choice. Possible slogans might be:

☺ I'm Drug Free   ☺ I Love My Body
☺ Choose Good Friends   ☺ Hang With The Right Folks
☺ Be The Best!

Have the students ask permission to display them in their rooms at home.

11. Acrostic Poetry
Write a class acrostic poem of No Alcohol.

N--
O--

A--
L--
C--
O--
H--
O--
L--

12. Journal Writing

If a child has been in foster care, he/she may be experiencing many feelings of guilt, insecurity, and anger. Explain that it's okay to have these feelings but the feelings can be helped by talking about them or writing them down. Encourage him/her to write his/her feelings in his/her journal. Insure him/her that no one will read the journal without permission.

13. Filling Pop's Shoes

This simple game is fun but emphasizes that children are not equipped to handle adult size problems. Each child needs his own shoes and a pair of shoes borrowed from his/her father or guardian. First the students race a predetermined distance in their own shoes. Then the students put on their father/guardian's shoes and race the same distance. If the shoes come off, the racers have to stop and put the shoes back on. After the race is complete, emphasize that children don't fit into adult-size shoes nor do they need to face adult-size problems. Emphasize the importance of telling a responsible adult when they are faced with a problem that seems too big for them.

14. Good Memory Clouds

Prepare a worksheet filled with only fluffy clouds. Explain to the students that in the story Savanna was going through some sad times and in sad times, it helps to hold on to happy memories. Have them fill each cloud with a good memory of an experience with their families. Smaller children might draw pictures of their memories in the clouds. (This could also be done on the bulletin board. Give each child one cloud and have him/her write his/her special memory. Then make a bulletin board display of all the memories.)

15. One and Only One

This activity provides an opportunity for every student to tell what makes them unique. Give each child a 3 by 5 file card. Ask them to write descriptions of themselves that tell something unique about themselves-- their accomplishments, their experiences, their interests--things that make them different from anyone else in the group. Ask them not to sign their names. Collect the cards and shuffle them. Let the students sit in a circle on the floor. Pass out the cards. If a child should get his/her own card, he/she selects another one. One by one the players read the cards and the group tries to guess who wrote it. The following are examples that might be written on cards:

I take dancing lessons.   **I can hit a free shot.**

I love peach ice cream.   **I am very friendly.**

16. Trust Toss

This game is intended to emphasize that we trust others to help us. Give the students 3 sheets of paper each. Tell them to write on each of the sheets of paper something they trust others to do such as:

A. I trust Mom to do the laundry.
B. I trust my friend to play with me.
C. I trust my sister to share.

Have them crumple up each written trust into a ball. Then have them gather around a trash can and take three giant steps backwards. On "go" have each student toss his/her trust balls toward the trash can and sit down. He/she is allowed only three tosses...one for each sheet. Read the trusts that made it into the trash can and talk about how important it is to trust people with these things. Then gather up the balls that missed, read them, and ask the students how they would feel if these trusts had to be broken.

17. Classroom Poetry

Help the students write a poster poem entitled "Home Is".

18. Social Service Interview

Invite a social service worker to come to speak with the class. Prior to him/her coming, help the class to formulate questions to ask him/her about his/her work. Allow the students to interview the worker.

Follow-up Tips For Parent(s)

A child separated from parents grieves for the missing parent(s) just as an adult grieves for a deceased parent. Being separated from parents may cause frustration and longing that makes a child frantic with grief. It is common for a child in this circumstance to take on the parent role toward other siblings as he/she attempts to cope with or mask his/her own feelings as Savanna did in this story (Voist, 1986).

1. Discuss the concept of foster care with your child. Let him/her know that in some situations children benefit from being placed in foster care while family problems are being resolved.

2. Talk about the problems that may necessitate foster care such as parental drug abuse, insufficient resources to provide life's necessities, mental or physical abuse, or illness of a parent, etc.

3. Assure your child of your love for him/her while emphasizing the importance of compassion toward others who may be in this situation.

4. Discuss Savanna's fears and how the Adams family helped her to deal with those fears.

5. Discuss the use of drugs and the effects of drug use on a family.

Story Eight
Buddy Was My Best Friend

Objectives

1. To help children understand that the bond between a person and a pet can be very special and that the death of a pet can bring the same emotions as the death of a person.

2. To help children understand that it is important to discuss their feelings about the loss of their pet with a parent or some other support person.

3. To help children understand the responsibility of caring for a pet.

4. To help children understand that an old, beloved pet cannot be replaced by the purchase of a new pet.

5. To help children develop a feeling of compassion toward another individual who has lost a pet.

Overview

On a very cold winter day Lorna finds a shivering puppy under the bushes by her back door. All efforts to find its owner prove to be futile. The puppy is adopted into the household and becomes a very special companion to Lorna. The two are inseparable. Buddy has one bad habit. He likes to chase tires. This habit cannot be broken and leads to Buddy's death. Lorna and her family bury Buddy but the memory of his love for her and her love for him continue far beyond his grave.

Discussion Questions

1. How would you describe Lorna's feelings on the day she found Buddy?

2. Tell about Lorna's parents.

3. What caused Buddy to die? Could anyone have stopped him?

4. Was it alright for Lorna to cry over a dog?

5. What would you tell Lorna to do to make herself feel better? How can her parents help her?

6. Will getting a new pet replace Buddy?

Suggested Activities

1. Many Loves

Talk with the students about many kinds of love. (Examples might be love of parent to parent, parent to child, sibling to sibling, friend to friend, person to pet, etc.) Discuss what each individual may do to show his/her love to the other individual.

2. Pets We Have

Invite the students to draw pictures of pets they have or would like to have. Have them write stories about their pets. Have them share their pictures and stories. Then display both the pictures and the stories in the classroom.

3. Pet Care

Talk about the things needed to care for a pet. Make a poster of the suggestions made. Be sure the students have mentioned teaching the pet obedience.

4. Feelings for Pets

Have the class share Lorna's feelings when she found Buddy. Compare her feelings with those of her parents.

5. Sharing Grief Feelings

Divide the class into groups of four students and allow them to share Lorna's feelings when Buddy died. Have them discuss in small groups things Lorna could do to help herself through this difficult time. After fifteen minutes, bring all the groups back together. Have the small groups share their suggestions of how Lorna could help herself. Make a poster of all the suggestions. (If someone mentions getting a new pet, be sure to lead the students to the understanding that this may be acceptable but that Buddy cannot be replaced.)

6. Making Sympathy Cards

Invite the students to design and color sympathy cards for Lorna. Then have them write a message of sympathy inside the card.

7. Sour Puss

Explain to the students that when someone feels very sad, sometimes it helps them if they giggle and act silly. Explain that they are going to play a silly game. Have the students sit in a circle. One student is IT and he/she stands in the center of the circle. He/she turns to one of the other students and asks a stupid question such as "Do horses have wings?" The student to whom the question is asked must answer by telling something that Lorna could do to make herself feel better. The answers must be very silly such as "Ride a baseball bat". The student who is answering the question is not allowed to smile. The student asking the questions may laugh and do all kinds of antics to try to get the other students to smile. The child who does smile must come to the center of the circle and replace the person who is IT. Explain to the students that this would not be appropriate when a child just learns of the death.

8. Fast Thinking

Each child has a pencil and paper. They are instructed to write down the first twelve words, relating to pets, that come to their minds after they receive the cue. Set a strict time limit for each word dependent upon the age of the children. Use words such as flea, puppy, bone, veterinarian, collar, bark, grave, or other pet related words. Have the students share their words. Much information can be received about the students' thoughts from this activity.

9. Create a Photo Album
For the child who has lost a pet, encourage him/her to search through family photographs and find pictures that include the pet. Have him/her use the pictures to make a photograph album in memory of his/her pet. If no photographs are available, he/she may choose to draw pictures of his/her pet with family members and include these in an album.

10. Pet Book Making
Have the child who is grieving for a pet write a story about the dead pet. Then, provide appropriate materials for book making. Allow the child to use his/her story to make a book about his/her pet. Children who are not grieving for a pet can join in this activity by writing about their pet or the pet they would like to own.

11. Poem Writing
Encourage the child grieving for a pet to remember his/her pet in poetry. This can be done individually or as a whole-class activity. A class poem should be written on chart paper and displayed in the room. The student working alone should be given the opportunity to share his/her poem and to write the completed poem on chart paper to display in the classroom.

12. Acrostic Writing
Help the students to write an acrostic poem about the deceased pet using the pet's name. This activity can be done alone, in small groups, or with the entire class. Display the work after it is shared. An example is as follows:
B - *Buddy was my best friend.*
U - *Under the bushes I did find him.*
D - *Dancing he did try.*
D - *Dinner was his special treat.*
Y - *You should have known him.*

13. Music Memories

Have the students lie on the carpet. Tell them that you are going to play some very restful music. As they listen very quietly to the music and lie still, they are to push all other thoughts from their minds and imagine themselves running through a meadow with their pets. Encourage them to feel the breeze blowing, smell the wildflowers, feel the rocks beneath their feet, feel the briar brush their leg, etc. This relaxation technique helps to relieve the stress felt by a grieving individual.

Follow-up Tips For Parent(s)

The loss of a pet can be a very traumatic experience for anyone but especially for a child. To make the child's grief "good grief", Sandra Fox in her book *Good Grief* says children must accomplish three things:

1. Understanding
2. Grieving
3. Commemorating

Be sure that the child has a clear statement about death and knows that the pet will not return and cannot be replaced by another pet. (Adame, 1996). These activities may be beneficial to the child grieving for a pet:

- Plan a short memorial service for the pet. Allow the child to help plan the service if he/she chooses to do so.

- If a photograph of the pet is available, display it as you do those of family members and friends.

- Talk with your child about the dead pet. Reinforce the idea that the animal will always be special and will remain in his/her memories.

- If a new pet is acquired, allow a waiting period and choose a different name for the new pet.

Death of a Classmate

Rocking, Rocking, Rocking

Objectives

1. To help children understand that the death of a sibling or close friend is a difficult time and that one may experience denial, fear, anger, depression, and confusion.

2. To lead children to understand that although serious illness and death occur most frequently in the elderly population, young people can also be affected.

3. To lead children to understand that denial of the diagnosis of a terminal illness is a common reaction and that some grief is experienced as one accepts his/her physical condition.

4. To help children determine that an individual living with a serious or terminal illness needs the comfort and companionship of friends as he/she battles the illness.

5. To help children understand that by reaching out and helping others, we help ourselves to heal from our own grief.

6. To stress to children that they may have friends of many ages.

Overview

Jeff, a second grade student develops a very close relationship with an elderly gentleman, Mr. Roxburgh. Mr. Roxburgh shares a testimony of his own faith and trust in God with Jeff. Shortly after this, Mr. Roxburgh dies and Jeff's family explains to him that his friend now lives with God.

Jeff's parents notice that he is not eating and discover that his stomach appears to be swollen. He is diagnosed with a very rare form of liver cancer. Chemotherapy treatments are begun. He continues his normal activities. The chemotherapy has the usual side effects of hair loss and tiredness but shrinks the cancer. Jeff becomes a possible candidate for a liver transplant. Classmates of Jeff organize a rock-a-thon to help raise money for travel expenses for Jeff's family. However, the cancer begins to grow again, more aggressively than ever. Jeff, unfortunately, does not get the liver transplant, but goes to join Mr. Roxburgh.

Discussion Questions

1. Who was Mr. Roxburgh? What words would you use to describe him?

2. Why was Jeff so tired and never hungry at the beginning of the story? Was Jeff sick because he did not eat?

3. Trish, Jeff's little sister, was not talked about much in the story. What do you think happened to her while Jeff was so sick? How do you think she felt when Jeff died?

4. Have you ever done anything to help someone who was sick? How did it make you feel?

5. Have you ever known anyone who died? If so, who was it? How did you feel? What helped you during that time?

Suggested Activities

1. Focus On Health Issues

Ask the students what they know about cancer and its treatment. Most of them will know someone who has had the illness. Allow them to share their knowledge. During this time help the children to see that they are different from Jeff, in the story, because he was very ill and they are healthy. Emphasize that cancer in children does happen but it is rare so they will not become overly anxious.

2. Analyze Emotions

After reading the book, put these names on the board–Mom, Dad, Trish, and Jeff. Reminding the children that these were the members of Jeff's family. Ask the students to supply words that would describe the feelings of these family members at the beginning, middle, and end of the story. Write the words under the name of the family member they think would be experiencing that emotion. If the children fail to mention anger, fear, tired, depressed or other appropriate words, supply them and allow them to talk about them.

3. The Human Body

Plan a unit of study on the human body and the function of the vital organs. Have the students locate the liver. If possible, have a preserved liver of an animal to share with the class. Talk about the possibility fo transplants for these vital organs and where the donations are obtained.

4. Hospital Visit

Arrange a field trip to a local hospital. Have the hospital arrange for a tour of the x-ray department.

5. Hospital Helpers

Adopt the children's ward of a local hospital. For the children's ward do the following things:

- Create artwork for the walls.
- Make cards for the children in the hospital.

- Write letters to the children in the hospital.
- Help the students plan and perform a short play or musical for the children in the hospital.

6. Special Grandparents

Point out to the students that just as Mr. Roxburgh was a special friend to Jeff in the story, older citizens often need young children to be special friends to them.

Arrange for the class to adopt special grandparents from a local nursing home. For the adopted grandparents have the children do these things:
A. Make cards and write letters to the senior adults.
B. Create artwork for the bulletin board at the nursing home.
C. Make special favors and deliver them to the nursing home for special occasions.
D. Arrange a field trip to the nursing home to meet the adopted grandparents.

7. Memory Pockets

If the students have experienced the death of a friend or relative, make a memory pocket for the bulletin board from construction paper. Have each child write a special memory of the deceased person on a slip of paper. Have them put their memory in the memory pocket. Remind them that the memory will always live in their minds. Students who wish to share their memory may be allowed to do so. Remind the students that sometimes our memories of deceased persons are not so good and if they have a bad memory, it is good to write it also.

8. Memory Board

Have the students draw and color pictures of the deceased person. Have them write stories or special memories about the person. Display the pictures and stories on a memory board in the classroom or in the hallway.

9. Shared Memories

Display a photograph of the deceased person. Have each student write one describing statement about the deceased person. Display the statements around the picture.

10. One Piece Missing

Use a sheet of twenty four by thirty six inch tagboard. Divide the tagboard into enough puzzle pieces for each class member to have one, including the deceased person. Cut the pieces apart. Allow the children to draw pictures of themselves in their puzzle piece. Put the puzzle back together adding the piece for the deceased person which will be blank. Label the puzzle as one piece of us is missing. Point out that although the person is gone, he/she will always be a part of us like the blank piece of puzzle--without it, the puzzle would not be complete.

11. Memorial Service

If the deceased person is a child or faculty member, plan a memorial service for the school. Allow the children who wish to do so to participate in the service by reading a poem, singing a song, etc. Conclude the service by planting a tree in memory of the deceased person.

12. Sympathy Cards

Allow the students to design and color sympathy cards for the family of the deceased person. Have them write messages in the cards and have them delivered.

13. Rock-A-Thon

Plan and conduct a rock-a-thon to benefit a critically ill child and his/her family. All you need is rocking chairs, a large area such as a gym or classroom, a few donated refreshments, and children willing to participate by collecting pledges. The students feel very good about being able to contribute to someone else.

14. Healthy Grief

Emphasize the importance of expressing our grief and some of the healthy ways to do so. Have prepared a cardboard beanstalk with premarked steps and a Jack to climb it. As the children are able to give one positive way to express grief, move Jack up the beanstalk to the next premarked step. When he has reached the top, reward the children with a small treat or sticker.

15. Brainy Math Problems

Make word problems to correlate with the story. Use these in a math center or as whole group activities. Some examples are as follows:

A. Sixteen boys rocked in the rock-a-thon. Fifteen girls rocked in the rock-a-thon. How many children rocked in all?

B. Twenty children are rocking in the rock-a-thon. Twelve of them do not have rocking chairs. How many of them do have rocking chairs?

C. The girls collected 26 pennies, 92 dimes, 151 nickels, 715 quarters, 20 fifty cent pieces, and 159 one dollar bills. How much money did they collect in all? (Allow the use of calculators.)

D. The rock-a-thon will start at 8:15. It will last for three hours. What time will it end?

E. There are 42 children in the rock-a-thon. Each will need 4 cookies for snack time. Mrs. Brown made three batches of cookies. Each batch made 56 cookies. Will that be enough cookies? How do you know?

Follow-up Tips For Parent(s)

Watch for teachable moments to introduce and discuss the concept of death with your child, preferably before the death of a family member or close friend. Nature itself offers a wide array of circumstances that can assist when teaching about death. Some of these are a dead animal by the roadside, a dead fish by the ocean, or a dead bird in the yard. The changing seasons illustrate the natural cycle of life. In spring the trees bud and bloom. In fall the leaves turn color and fall to the ground. Over time the decaying leaves decompose and become part of the soil. These provide nourishment for the new life that we observe the following spring. (Voist, 1986)

1. Ask your child if any parts of the story made him/her sad. If so, which parts?

2. Ask your child if any parts of the story made him/her happy. If so, which parts?

3. Share with your child your beliefs about life after death.

Death of a Parent

The Fresh Earth

Objectives

1. To help children understand that the loss of a parent is very traumatic and the healing process may take a long time.

2. To help the child understand that he/she may experience many emotions such as depression, anger, fear, confusion, and guilt and that it is acceptable to experience these emotions.

3. To help the child recognize the need for a support system when dealing with his/her grief and to help him/her discover who that support system can be.

4. To help the child realize that when experiencing grief over the loss of a loved one, he/she may make some poor decisions.

5. To help the child realize that death does not make an individual perfect. In our memories, we remember both the good and bad qualities of the deceased.

Overview

Heather's family has just received the sad news that her father has been killed in an automobile accident. Heather refuses to accept that her father is not returning home to his family. In an attempt to reach Heather, her grandmother shares a story that she wrote about her own memories on the day her own father was buried. The grandmother's story begins with why she smells the fresh earth on a bitter January day. The smell of the fresh dirt revives her memories. The memories take her back to her childhood. She recalls how her father and mother instruct the young children in her family in the planting, cultivating, and harvesting of the Irish potato. As the story concludes, her thoughts return to the present and the cemetery where she and other family members are returning her father, an avid gardener, to the earth. Grandmother reminds Heather that she can always see her father in her memories and that it is okay to talk to him. The story concludes with Heather telling about her dream of her father.

Discussion Questions

1. What has happened to Heather's father?

2. How did Heather react to the news of her father's death?

3. Why do you think Heather's grandmother shared her story with Heather?

4. Where was Heather's grandmother at the beginning of the story? Why was she smelling the fresh earth?

5. Why do you think memories are important to us?

Suggested Activities

1. **Life Cycle of Plants**
   Invite the students to share their knowledge of the planting season. Emphasize that seeds need the warmth of the sun, good soil, and water for germination to occur. Emphasize that not all plants come from seeds. Emphasize the life cycle of a plant.

2. **Preparing for the Story**
   Allow the students to examine the tuber of the Irish potato, calling attention to the small indentions called eyes. Ask them to speculate what will come from the eyes of the tuber. (Some students may have had experience with potato sprouts. It will be helpful to have a sprouted potato to show.)

3. **Character Emotions**
   Read the book to the class or allow students to read alone, depending on the child's reading level. After the reading is complete, guide the students to explain who the storyteller is, the age of the storyteller, the age of the gardener, the setting of the story, and what is happening. Have the students compare the emotions of the storyteller at different points in the story.

4. **Human Life Cycle**
   Ask the students what they think it means to die. Allow them to discuss their feelings but stress that death is final, not reversible. Talk about the age of the gardener in the story and how the aging process affects individuals. (Examples might be glasses, wrinkles, gray hair, bald-headed, rounder bodies, slower walk, splotchy skin, etc.)

5. **What Is Dead?**
   The teacher begins, "I am alive, I can breathe." As each child is given a turn, he/she adds another part such as, "I am alive, I can sit." Allow each student to have a turn to tell one thing that he/she can do. Then the teacher says, "When you are dead, you cannot do these things."

6. **Alive, Inanimate, Or Dead**

Take a walk outside and have the students touch different things such as grass, leaves, sticks, or bugs that are dead or alive. Ask, "Are they alive?" Ask if they have ever touched a dead animal or bug. If so, how did it feel? Point out that death is not dirty but if they touch dead animals, even bugs, they need to remember to wash their hands to remove bacteria.

7. **Funeral Home Tour (For Upper Elementary Grades 3-5)**

Discuss with the students what happens to a human body after death. Most students will know about a funeral home. Arrange a tour of the local funeral home. Be sure to tell the person conducting the tour that the students will not see dead bodies. Prior to the visit, allow the students to prepare a list of questions for the mortician. Ask him/her to share with the students the different kinds of funeral services they conduct.

8. **Cemetery Visit (For Upper Elementary Grades 3-5)**

Visit a nearby cemetery. Point out the different sizes of graves, grave markers, and mausoleums. Allow students to read the epitaphs and discuss their meanings. Have the students read the dates of birth and death on the markers. Have the students find the person who was oldest when he/she died and the person who was youngest.

9. **Words About Death**

Help the children make a list of words they hear when people are talking about death. Discuss these until a definition is formed for each. Write the word and its definition onto a chart in the classroom. Use these words to make a crossword puzzle or a word search activity.

10. **Reliving Memories**

Invite the students to share memories of persons they have known who have died. Allow them to express the emotions they felt. Stress the importance of sharing these feelings. Then ask the students to draw pictures of the person they remembered and write a story about that person. Display the stories and pictures in the classroom.

11. "Death Benefits" Interview (For Upper Elementary Grades 3-5)

Have the students interview family members to discover their beliefs related to death. Allow the students to help make the list of questions for the interview. Allow them to take the questions home, interview a predetermined number of adults, and return their answers to class. Provide time for sharing the answers they received. (This should be preceded by a letter to parent(s)s stressing that beliefs will not be judged, only discussed.)

12. Remember the Good Things I Did

Often a grieving child feels guilty for things they did not do for a deceased loved one. This game focuses on the good things they did. The leader starts with a simple statement such as, "I'm glad I brought him the paper." Then the other children take turns recalling the good things they did for the deceased (Fitzgerald, 1992).

13. Don't Let One Hit the Floor

Have the students write secret messages for the deceased on little slips of paper. Roll the paper slips up and put them in balloons. Blow the balloons up and tie them off. Then play, "Don't let one hit the floor." Children try to keep all the balloons afloat. After a little while, stop the game and give one child a pin. Ask him/her to pop the balloon he/she is holding and read the message. One by one the balloons are popped and the messages are read by whomever is holding the balloon. This helps the children not have to claim their own secrets unless they so desire (Fitzgerald, 1992).

14. Balloon Release

Have the students write secret messages for the deceased. Put the messages in balloons, fill the balloons with helium, tie the balloons off. Then allow the students to release the balloons taking their secret messages far, far, away.

15. Heavenly Puppets

Give each child a brown paper bag. Instruct them to make people puppets. When the puppets are complete, divide the class into teams of twos. One member of each team uses his/her puppet to represent a deceased person and the other team member uses his/her puppet to represent a person who is alive. The person with the living puppet interviews the deceased puppet to ask questions about death and heaven. The person with the deceased puppet answers the questions. This can give adults an opportunity to suggest realistic answers (Fitzgerald, 1992).

16. Express Your Anger

Death can cause anger. Physical activity is a wonderful release for anger. Give the child a punching bag, old pillow, or large cardboard box. Allow them to punch out their emotions. Encourage them to shout out their thoughts as they punch such as, "I hate you for leaving. I am so mad at you."

17. Tape Your Anger

Give the grieving, angry child a tape recorder. Ask him/her to speak into the recorder any feelings he/she is having about the deceased person or things he/she did to the person, or things he/she wishes he/she had done for the person. Then have the child listen and think about the words. Have him/her erase the tape recorder. Stress at the beginning that no one else will hear these words.

18. Written Anger

For students who show anger about the death of a loved one, give them a large sheet of paper. Have them start writing down all the names of persons who have made them angry. As they write the names of the persons, encourage them to discuss what the person did to make them angry. When they are finished, ask them what they want to do with the names. Encourage them to tear them up and get rid of them. Tell them that now they have gotten rid of the anger. Lead them to share their feelings now. They should feel lighter (Fitzgerald, 1992).

19. Journal Writing

Writing is a wonderful tool for expressing anger. Allow the grieving child to keep a journal. Assure him/her that no one will read the journal without permission. Encourage him/her to tell exactly how he/she feels each day. Invite them to find one person they can trust to share these feelings.

20. Death In Different Cultures

For older students, divide the class into teams and assign each team a culture to research the customs for dealing with death in that culture. (Examples might be Americans, Native Americans, Romans, Egyptians, Chinese, etc.)

Follow-up Tips For Parent(s)

Children have many questions about the mystery of death, just as adults. We need to help them by speaking openly and frankly to them. We must let them know that we do not have all the answers but that we are willing to listen and help them find answers if possible.

Suggestions For Each Story

1. Let your child retell the story in his/her own words. Be sure that he/she understands that the planting of potatoes was in the author's memory.

2. Discuss with your child the feelings of the author of the story and Heather in the story and the reasons for these feelings.

3. If your child has been associated with someone who has died, ask him/her to share his/her memories of the deceased person. At this time, you may like to share your own memories of the deceased individual with your child.

Bibliography

Adame, C. (1996) *When your pet dies*. New York, NY : Berkley Books.

Anderson, K., & Carlson, M. (1967) *Games for all occassions*. Grand Rapids, MI: Zandervan Publishing House.

Attig, T. (1996) *How we grieve: Relearning the world*. New York, NY: Oxford University Press.

Bank, S. P. & Kahn, M. D. (1982) *The sibling bond*. New York, NY: Basic Books.

Beckman, R. (1990) *Children who grieve*. Holmes Beach, FL: Learning Publications.

Bloomquist, G. M. (1990) *Coping as a foster child*. New York, NY: The Rosen Publishing Group.

Childs, E. (1992) *Good grief rituals*. Barrytown, NY: Station Hill Press.

Clapp, G. (1992) *Divorce and new beginnings*. New York, NY : John Wiley and Sons.

Fitzgerald, H. (1992) *The grieving child*. Hamden, CT : Fireside.

Fry, V. L. (1995) *Part of me died, too*. New York, NY: Dutton Children's Books.

Gaffney, D. (1988) *Seasons of grief, helping your child grow through loss*. New York, NY: New American Library.

Gregson, B. (1982) *The incredible indoor game book*. Torrance, CA: Fearon Teacher Aids.

Grollman, E. A. (1993) *Straight talk about death for teenagers*. Boston, MA : Beacon Press.

Huntley, T. (1991) *Helping children grieve*. Minneapolis, MN: Augsburg Fortress.

McCasland, J. (1997) *100 indoor games for school kids*. Colorado Springs, CO: Cook Ministry Resources.

Rando, T. A. (1998) *How to go on living when someone you love dies*. Lexington, MA: Lexington Books.

Rugg, S. (1995) *Memories live forever*. Marietta, GA: Rising Sun Center For Loss and Renewal.

Ross, E. K. (1993) *On children and death*. New York, NY: Macmillan Publishing Company.

Salk, L. (1979) *Dear dr. salk: Answers to your questions about your family*. New York, NY: Harper and Rowe.

Seilbert, D., Drolet, J. C. & Fetro, J. V. *Are you sad too? Helping children deal with loss and death*. Santa Cruz, CA: EtR Associates.

Viorst, J. (1988) *Necessary losses*. New York, NY: Simon and Schuster.